The Captive

Mary Rowlandson

The True Story of the Captivity of
Mrs. Mary Rowlandson Among the Indians
and God's Faithfulness to her in her Time of Trial

Introduction by Mark Ludwig

American Eagle Publications, Inc.
Tucson, Arizona 85717

Published in the United States jn 1990 by
American Eagle Publications, Inc.
Post Office Box 41401
Tucson, Arizona 85717

Originally published in Cambridge, Massachusetts in 1682
by Samuel Green under the title
*The Soverignty and Goodness of God, Together with the Faithfulness of
His Promises Displayed, Being a Narrative of the Captivity and
Restoration of Mrs. Mary Rowlandson.*

Map on page 4 by Brian Cary; illustrations on pages 20 and 45 cour-
tesy of The Trustees of the Boston Public Library.

Library of Congress Cataloging-in-Publication Data

Rowlandson, Mary White, ca. 1635-1678.
   The Captive.

   Originally published under title: The soveraighty & goodness of God.
   1. Rowlandson, Mary White, ca. 1635-ca. 1678. 2. Indians of North
America—Massachusetts—Captivities. 3. Indians of North America—
Massachusetts—Biography. 4. Indians of North America—
Massachusetts—History— Colonial period, ca. 1600-1775. 5. King
Phillip's War, 1675-1676.   I. Title
E87.R895R69   1988   973.2'4 [B]   88-24037
ISBN 0-929408-03-9

Printed in the United States of America

Introduction

Although little known today, this story was once widely regarded as a classic of American literature. First published in 1682, it has seen over forty editions in the past three centuries, and it marked the beginning of a very popular and uniquely American form of literature, the so-called "captivity narrative" which was the predecessor of the American "Western". This book also holds a prominent place in women's literature since it is the first full length work published in America which was authored by a woman.

Mary Rowlandson's narrative is the true story of her capture by the Indians in a bloody massacre and of her service as their slave for three months in the middle of a New England wilderness winter. It is an arresting and exciting book. Yet it is not the story line or the excitement that won this narrative its enduring fame. Mary Rowlandson's is a story of amazing faith and perseverance in the face of adversity, and a great testimony to the faithfulness of God.

The fathers of our nation understood faith and perseverance only too well. Many came to America so that they could live their lives and serve God as they sincerely believed He wanted them to. They chose to brave a fierce wilderness rather than allow their faith to be choked by a government that had a different agenda for their lives. Other generations were caught up in sweeping revivals of the faith, like the Great Awakening, and they put that faith to work applying Christian principles to government, caring for the poor, and taking Christ to the lost in America and around the world. And from the Pilgrims—who lost half their number in the first year—to the men who laid down their lives in the revolutionary war, the people of this nation knew suffering. Some suffered of their own choosing for what they believed in. Others were afflicted against their will, whether by war, by want, or by pestilence.

Mary Rowlandson spoke to such men and women. They could commune with her in suffering and hardship, and they could take courage in their own trials as they read about how God upheld her. By every measure, Mary Rowlandson was real to her readers. She was not some great warrior who stood shoulders above other men, or a Christian zealot martyred for her brilliant and daring witness. She was an ordinary person. She did not hide her doubts, her anguish, her fear and her weaknesses. She did not put on the airs of a false religiosity which she did not live. When she saw something that made her angry, like a hypocritical Christian Indian, she let her readers know what she thought in no uncertain terms—even if it might sound harsh to tender ears. Yet she also spoke of her own hypocricies and confesses that she thought she deserved to suffer. When a small kindness was shown to her, she openly expressed her sincere and humble gratitude. And when she looked back on her experience, she marveled that she did not lose her mind.

Although our nation has become renowned the world over as a place of peace and prosperity, and although many no longer profess Christ, Mary Rowlandson still has something to say to us. Life is still troublesome as ever, and none of us is without difficulties. The challenge to live a productive and meaningful life is perhaps even greater than it was three centuries ago. Mary Rowlandson is one who might well encourage us in the midst of our troubles. What are our afflictions compared with hers? And even if one of us is facing immediate death, her testimony rings clear across the centuries to assure us that no matter how deep the waters we must pass through, no matter how great the trials we must face, God will give us what we need to accomplish what He has called us to.

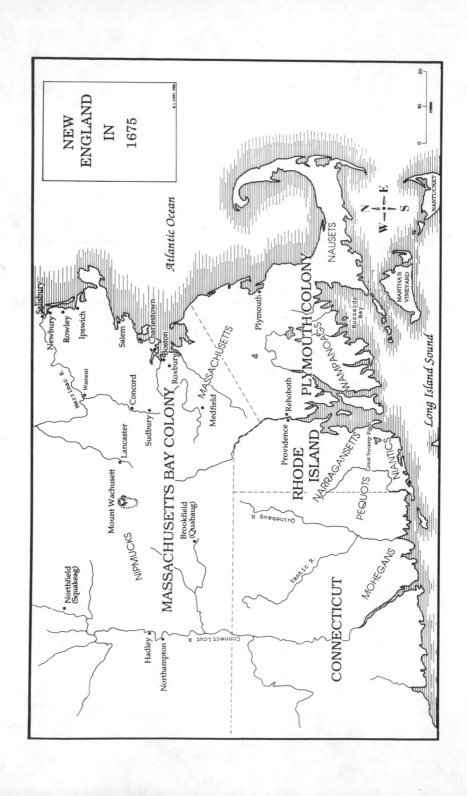

NEW
ENGLAND
IN
1675

B.L. CARY 1988

0   10   20
miles

N
W — E
S

Atlantic Ocean

Long Island Sound

Salisbury
Newbury
Rowley
Ipswich
Merrimac R.
Wamesit
Salem
Charlestown
Boston
Roxbury
Concord
Sudbury
Medfield
Lancaster
Mount Wachusett
Brookfield
(Quabaug)
Northfield
(Squakeag)
Hadley
Northampton
Connecticut R.

MASSACHUSETTS BAY COLONY
MASSACHUSETTS
NIPMUCKS
CONNECTICUT

Plymouth
PLYMOUTH COLONY
NAUSETS
MARTHA'S
VINEYARD
NANTUCKET
Buzzards
Bay
WAMPANOAGS
Providence
Rehoboth
RHODE
ISLAND
NARRAGANSETTS
Great Swamp Fight
NIANTICS
PEQUOTS
Quinebaug R.
Yantic R.
MOHEGANS

Setting the Scene

Little is known of Mary Rowlandson apart from what she tells us in her book. She was probably born in England in 1635, the daughter of one of the original proprietors of Lancaster, Massachusetts, John White. She married the Rev. Joseph Rowlandson in Lancaster around 1656 and continued there until it was sacked in 1676, one of the many frontier communities which fell prey to the Indians in a war known to historians as King Phillip's War.

In retrospect, this war seemed almost inevitable. In the early days of the New England settlements, many had high hopes of evangelizing the Indians and leading them to Christ. The colonists supported missionaries and eagerly trained willing converts in the faith. Often these Christian Indians lived among the colonists or in special communities of their own. They elected their own leaders, obeyed the laws of the colonies, and were generally grafted into civilized society. However, not all of the Indians were willing to accept the faith of Christ or the government of the English colonies.

On the other hand, the puritans of the seventeenth century were not about to adopt a pluralistic statism in which the Indians and their heathen customs and morals were given co-equal status with Christian government. Instead, all were subject to the laws of the colony, colonist and Indian, Christian and heathen alike. These laws regulated everything from thievery to blasphemy, Sabbath breaking, and property rights, including many things which were foreign to the Indians. This situation understandably proved to be irritating to the Indians at times. More than that, though, the Indians were coming to see that their old ways of life were inevitably coming to an end, and many, especially the Sachems and Powaws, the leaders and medicine men, were not willing to change simply because the English expected them to do so. These were seeds enough for a conflict.

Open hostility began in 1675 after ten years of deteriorating relations between Plymouth Colony and an ambitious young Wampanoag Sachem, Phillip. Under the leadership of Phillip, the Wampanoags grew bolder and more independent. They came to be perceived as a threat to the colonies, and not without reason. On a number of occasions information came to the colonial authorities concerning Phillip's plans for a revolt, or concerning contact he had made with the Dutch and the French, England's bitter enemies. While it is impossible to determine how much truth there was to such reports, Phillip was once cornered attempting to deceive the English when he was questioned about his activities, which naturally tended to confirm the worst suspicions.

On January 29, 1675 the Christian Indian John Sassamon, a former aide of Phillip's, was mysteriously murdered and thrown into a frozen pond to hide the deed. He had recently informed the authorities in Plymouth that Phillip was organizing a general revolt against the English. His warnings went unheeded until his willingness to speak against Phillip cost him his life. Later, an eye witness stepped forward leading to the arrest of three suspects—Wampanoags. They were hanged on June 8, 1675 after a unanimous conviction by a jury consisting of both Englishmen and Indians. After this, war became certain, and on June 24, the Wampanoags besieged the town of Swansea, killing 11 men.

At first, other tribes were not entirely willing to join Phillip in his war, although many were not about to pledge their loyalty to the English. The majority preferred to watch the battle from the sidelines for a while, to see if the Wampanoags had any chance of success. As Phillip and his warriors proved to be more than a match for the inexperienced colonial armies raised to fight him, he was able to enlist the help of the Nipmucks and the large Narraganset tribe. Many Indians who had been friendly to the English defected into Phillip's camp. However, several tribes, most notably the Mohegans, the Pequots, and the Niantics, remained loyal to the English, and even fought side by side with them.

During the first six months of the war, town after town succumbed to the Indians, and the death toll climbed into the hundreds. After a major offensive by the colonial army in December in the Great Swamp of Rhode Island, the fighting lulled as the Indians fled and regrouped to the north in Massachusetts. Nervousness prevailed. No one knew where the Indians would strike next, or when.

In January, two Christian Indians, James Quannapohit and Job Kattenanit, went among the hostile Indians as spies, trying to learn of their war plans. James Quannapohit returned on January 24 with news that the Indians were boasting about attacking Lancaster. Few measures were taken by the government to prevent such an attack, so pastor Joseph Rowlandson went to Boston on behalf of Lancaster to plead with the Council for help. On the evening of February 9, 1676 the other spy, Job Kattenanit, appeared at Captain Daniel Gookin's door in Cambridge to inform him that four hundred enemy warriors were at that moment on their way to attack Lancaster. The army was quickly assembled and the race to Lancaster was on.

Assault and Capture

On the tenth of February, 1675, came the Indians with great numbers upon Lancaster. Their first coming was about sun-rising. Hearing the noise of some guns, we looked out: several houses were burning, and the smoke ascending to heaven. There were five persons taken in one house. The father, the mother, and a sucking child they knockt on the head, the other two they took and carried away alive. There were two others who, being out of their garrison upon some occasion, were set upon. One was knockt on the head, the other escaped. Another there was who, running along, was shot and wounded, and fell down. He begged of them his life, promising them money (as they told me) but they would not hearken to him, but knockt him in head, and stript him naked, and split open his bowels. Another, seeing many of the Indians about his barn, ventured and went out, but was quickly shot down. There were three others belonging to the same garrison who were killed. The Indians, getting up upon the roof of the barn, had advantage to shoot down upon them over their fortification. Thus these murderous wretches went on, burning and destroying before them,

At length they came and beset our own house, and quickly it was the dolefullest day that ever mine eyes saw. The house stood upon the edge of a hill; some of the Indians got behind the hill, others into the barn, and others behind any thing that could shelter them, from all which places they shot against the house, so that the bullets seemed to fly like hail, and quickly they wounded one man among us, then another, and then a third. About two hours (according to my observation in that amazing time) they had been about the house before they prevailed to fire it (which they did with flax and hemp which they brought out of the barn). There being no defence about the house, only two flankers at two opposite corners, and one of them not finished, they fired it once, and one ventured out and quenched it, but they quickly fired it again, and that took. Now is that dreadfull hour come, that I have often heard of (in time of war, as it was the case of others) but now mine eyes see it. Some

in our house were fighting for their lives, others wallowing in their blood, the house on fire over our heads, and the bloody heathen ready to knock us on the head if we stirred out. Now might we hear mothers & children crying out for themselves, and one another, "Lord, what shall we do?"

I took my children (and one of my sisters, hers) to go forth and leave the house, but as soon as we came to the door and appeared, the Indians shot so thick that the bullets rattled against the house, as if one had taken a handfull of stones and thrown them, so that we were fain to give back. We had six stout dogs belonging to our garrison, but none of them would stir, though another time, if any Indian had come to the door, they were ready to fly upon him and tear him down. The Lord hereby would make us the more to acknowledge His hand, and to see that our help is always in Him. But out we must go, the fire increasing, and coming along behind us, roaring, and the Indians gaping before us with their guns, spears, and hatchets, to devour us.

No sooner were we out of the house, but my brother in law (being before wounded, in defending the house, in or near the throat) fell down dead, whereat the Indians scornfully shouted, and howled, and were presently upon him, stripping off his clothes. The bullets flying thick, one went through my side, and the same (as would seem) through the bowels and hand of my dear child in my arms. One of my elder sister's children, named William, had his leg broken, which the Indians perceiving, they knockt him on head. Thus were we butchered by those merciless heathen, standing amazed, with the blood running down to our heels. My eldest sister being yet in the house, and seeing those woeful sights, the infidels haling mothers one way, and children another, and some wallowing in their blood, and her elder son telling her that her son William was dead, and myself was wounded, she said, "and Lord, let me dy with them," which was no sooner said, but she was struck with a bullet, and fell down dead over the threshold. I hope she is reaping the fruit of her good labours, being faithfull to the service of God in her place. In her younger years she lay under much trouble upon spiritual accounts, till it pleased God to make that precious scripture take hold of her heart, 2 Corinthians 12:9, "And he said unto me, my grace is sufficient for thee." More than twenty years after, I have heard her tell how sweet and comfortable that place was to her. But to return: the Indians laid hold of us, pulling me one way, and the children another, and said, "Come, go along with us." I told them

they would kill me; they answered, if I were willing to go along
with them, they would not hurt me.

Oh! the dolefull sight that now was to behold at this house!
Come, behold the works of the Lord, what desolations he has made
in the earth. Of thirty seven persons who were in this one house,
none escaped either present death, or a bitter captivity, save only
one, who might say as he in Job 1:15: "And I only am escaped to
tell the news." There were twelve killed, some shot, some stab'd
with their spears, some knock'd down with their hatchets. When
we are in prosperity, oh the little that we think of such dreadfull
sights, and to see our dear friends and relations ly bleeding out their
heart-blood upon the ground. There was one who was chopt into
the head with a hatchet, and stript naked, and yet was crawling up
and down. It is a solemn sight to see so many Christians lying in
their blood, some here, and some there, like a company of sheep
torn by wolves, all of them stript naked by a company of hell-
hounds, roaring, singing, ranting, and insulting, as if they would
have torn our very hearts out. Yet the Lord by His almighty power
preserved a number of us from death, for there were twenty-four of
us taken alive and carried captive.

I had often before this said, that if the Indians should come, I
should choose rather to be killed by them, than taken alive, but when
it came to the tryal, my mind changed, Their glittering weapons so
daunted my spirit, that I chose rather to go along with those (as I
may say) ravenous bears, then that moment to end my dayes. And
that I may the better declare what happened to me during that
grievous captivity, I shall particularly speak of the several removes
we had up and down the wilderness.

The First Remove

Now away we must go with those barbarous creatures, with
our bodies wounded and bleeding, and our hearts no less than our
bodies. About a mile we went that night, up upon a hill within sight
of the town where they intended to lodge. There was hard by a

vacant house (deserted by the English before, for fear of the Indians). I asked them whither I might not lodge in the house that night, to which they answered, "What, will you love English men still?" This was the dolefullest night that ever my eyes saw. Oh the roaring, and singing, and dancing, and yelling of those black creatures in the night, which made the place a lively resemblance of hell. And as miserable was the waste that was there made, of horses, cattle, sheep, swine, calves, lambs, roasting pigs, and fowl, (which they had plundered in the town) some roasting, some lying and burning, and some boyling, to feed our merciless enemies, who were joyful enough though we were disconsolate. To add to the dolefulness of the former day, and the dismalness of the present night, my thoughts ran upon my losses and sad bereaved condition. All was gone, my husband gone, (at least separated from me, he being in the bay, and to add to my grief, the Indians told me they would kill him as he came homeward) my children gone, my relations and friends gone, our house and home and all our comforts within door, and without, all was gone, except my life, and I knew not but the next moment that might go too. There remained nothing to me but one poor wounded babe, and it seemed at present worse than death, that it was in such a pitiful condition, bespeaking compassion, and I had no refreshing for it, nor suitable things to revive it. Little do many think what is the savageness and brutishness of this barbarous enemy, even those that seem to profess more than others among them, when the English have fallen into their hands.

Those seven that were killed at Lancaster the summer before upon a Sabbath day, and the one that was afterward killed upon a week day, were slain and mangled in a barbarous manner, by one-ey'd John, and Marlborough's Praying Indians, which Captain Moseley brought to Boston, as the Indians told me.

The Second Remove

But now, the next morning, I must turn my back upon the town, and travel with them into the vast and desolate wilderness, I knew not whither. It is not my tongue nor pen can express the sorrows of my heart, and bitterness of my spirit, that I had at this departure. But God was with me in a wonderfull manner, carrying me along and bearing up my spirit, that it did not quite fail. One of the Indians carried my poor wounded babe upon a horse. It went moaning all along, I shall dy, I shall dy. I went on foot after it, with sorrow that cannot be expressed. At length I took it off the horse and carried it in my arms till my strength failed, and I fell down with it. Then they set me upon a horse with my wounded child in my lap and, there being no furniture upon the horse back, as we were going down a steep hill, we both fell over the horses head, at which they like inhumane creatures laughed, and rejoyced to see it, though I thought we should there have ended our dayes, as overcome with so many difficulties. But the Lord renewed my strength still, and carried me along, that I might see more of His power. Yea, so much that I could never have thought of it, had I not experienced it.

After this it quickly began to snow, and when night came on they stopt. And now I must sit in the snow by a little fire, and a few boughs behind me, with my sick child in my lap, and calling much for water, being now through the wound fallen into a violent fever. My own wound also grew so stiff that I could scarce sit down or rise up, yet so it must be, that I must sit all this cold winter night upon the cold snowy ground, with my sick child in my arms, looking that every hour would be the last of its life, and having no Christian friend near me, either to comfort or help me. Oh, I may see the wonderfull power of God, that my spirit did not utterly sink under my affliction. Still the Lord upheld me with His gracious and mercifull Spirit, and we were both alive to see the light of the next morning.

The Third Remove

The morning being come, they prepared to go on their way. One of the Indians got up on a horse and they set me up behind him, with my poor sick babe in my lap. A very wearisome and tedious day I had of it, what with my own wound, and my child being so exceedingly sick, and in a lamentable condition with her wound. It may be easily judged what a poor, feeble condition we were in, there being not the least crumb of refreshing that came within either of our mouths from Wednesday night to Saturday night, except only a little cold water. This day in the afternoon, about an hour by sun, we came to the place where they intended, viz., an Indian town called Wenimesset, northward of Quabaug. When we were come, oh the number of pagans (now merciless enemies) that there came about me, that I may say as David, Psalm 27:13. "I had fainted, unless I had believed," etc.

The next day was the Sabbath. I then remembered how careless I had been of God's holy time, how many Sabbaths I had lost and mispent, and how evily I had walked in God's sight, which lay so close unto my spirit that it was easie for me to see how righteous it was with God to cut off the thread of my life, and cast me out of His presence forever. Yet the Lord still shewed mercy to me and upheld me, and as He wounded me with one hand, so He healed me with the other.

This day there came to me one Robert Pepper (a man belonging to Roxbury) who was taken in Captain Beers' fight, and had now been a considerable time with the Indians, and up with them almost as far as Albany to see King Phillip, as he told me, and was now very lately come into these parts. Hearing, I say, that I was in this Indian town, he obtained leave to come and see me. He told me, he himself was wounded in the leg at Captain Beers' fight, and was not able some time to go, but as they carried him, and as he took Oaken leaves and laid to his wound, and through the blessing of God, he was able to travel again. Then I took Oaken leaves and laid them to my side, and with the blessing of God it cured me also. Yet before the cure was wrought, I may say, as it is in Psalm 38:5,6. "My wounds stink and are corrupt, I am troubled, I am bowed down greatly, I go mourning all the day long."

I sat much alone with a poor wounded child in my lap, which moaned night and day, having nothing to revive her body, or cheer her spirits. But instead of that, sometimes one Indian would come and tell me one hour, that "Your master will knock your child in the head," and then a second, and then a third, "Your master will quickly knock your child in the head." This was all the comfort I had from them, miserable comforters are ye all, as he said.

Thus nine dayes I sat upon my knees, with my babe in my lap, till my flesh was raw again. My child being even ready to depart this sorrowfull world, they bade me carry it out to another wigwam (I suppose because they would not be troubled with such spectacles) whither I went with a very heavy heart, and down I sat with the picture of death in my lap. About two hours in the night my sweet babe, like a lambe, departed this life, on February 18, 1675, it being about six years and five months old. It was nine dayes from the first wounding in this miserable condition, without any refreshing of one nature or other, except a little cold water. I cannot but take notice, how at another time I could not bear to be in the room where any dead person was, but now the case is changed. I must, and could ly down by my dead babe, side by side, all the night after. I have thought since of the wonderfull goodness of God to me, in preserving me in the use of my reason and senses in that distressed time, that I did not use wicked and violent means to end my own miserable life. In the morning when they understood that my child was dead, they sent for me home to my master's wigwam. (By my master in this writing must be understood Quanopin, who was a Saggamore, and married King Phillip's wife's sister, not that he first took me, but I was sold to him by another Narrhaganset Indian, who took me when first I came out of the garrison.) I went to take up my dead child in my arms to carry it with me, but they bid me let it alone. There was no resisting, but go I must and leave it. When I had been at my master's wigwam, I took the first opportunity I could get to go look after my dead child. When I came I askt them what they had done with it. Then they told me it was upon the hill. Then they went and shewed me where it was, where I saw the ground was newly digged, and there they told me they had buried it. There

I left that child in the wilderness, and must commit it, and my self also, in this wilderness- condition, to Him who is above all.

God having taken away this dear child, I went to see my daughter Mary, who was at this same Indian town at a wigwam not very far off, though we had little liberty or opportunity to see one another. She was about ten years old, & was taken from the door at first by a praying Indian & afterward sold for a gun. When I came in sight, she would fall a weeping, at which they were provoked, and would not let me come near her, but bade me be gone, which was a heart- cutting word to me. I had one child dead, another in the wilderness I knew not where, the third they would not let me come near to. "Me," as he said, "have ye bereaved of my children. Joseph is not, and Simeon is not, and ye will take Benjamin also; all these things are against me." I could not sit still in this condition, but kept walking from one place to another. And as I was going along, my heart was even overwhelm'd with the thoughts of my condition, that I should have children, and a nation which I knew not ruled over them. Whereupon I earnestly entreated the Lord, that He would consider my low estate, and shew me a token for good, and if it were His blessed will, some sign and hope of some relief.

And indeed quickly the Lord answered, in some measure, my poor prayers, for as I was going up and down mourning and lamenting my condition, my son came to me and asked me how I did. I had not seen him before, since the destruction of the town, and I knew not where he was, till I was informed by himself, that he was amongst a smaller parcel of Indians, whose place was about six miles off. With tears in his eyes, he asked me whether his sister Sarah was dead, and told me he had seen his sister Mary, and prayed me, that I would not be troubled in reference to himself.

The occasion of his coming to see me at this time, was this: There was, as I said, about six miles from us, a small plantation of Indians, where it seems he had been during his captivity. And at this time there were some forces of the Indians gathered out of our company, and some also from them (among whom was my son's master), to go to the assault and burn Medfield. In this time of the absence of his master, his dame brought him to see me. I took this to be some gracious answer to my earnest and unfeigned desire. The next day, viz. to this, the Indians returned from Medfield. All the company, and those that belonged to the other small company, came through the town that now we were at, but before they came to us, oh! the outrageous roaring and hooping that there was. They began their din about a mile before they came to us. By their noise and hooping they signified how many they had destroyed (which was at that time twenty-three.) Those that were with us at home, were gathered together as soon as they heard the hooping, and every time that the other went over their number, these at home gave a shout, that the very earth rang again. And thus they continued till those that had been upon the expedition were come up to the Saggamores' wigwam. And then, oh, the hideous insulting and triumphing that there was over some Englishmen's scalps that they had taken (as their manner is) and brought with them.

I cannot but take notice of the wonderfull mercy of God to me in those afflictions, in sending me a Bible. One of the Indians that came from Medfield fight, had brought some plunder, came to me and asked me if I would have a Bible. He had got one in his basket. I was glad of it, and asked him whether he thought the Indians would let me read. He answered, yes, so I took the Bible, and in that melancholy time, it came into my mind to read first the 28th Chapter of Deuteronomy, which I did, and when I had read it, my dark heart wrought on this manner, that there was no mercy for me, that the blessings were gone and the curses came in their room, and that I had lost my opportunity. But the Lord helped me still to go on reading till I came to Chapter 30, the seven first verses, where I found, there was mercy promised again, if we would return to Him by repentance, and though we were scattered from one end of the earth to the other, yet the Lord would gather us together, and turn all those curses upon our enemies. I do not desire to live to forget this scripture, and what comfort it was to me.

Now the Indians began to talk of removing from this place, some one way, and some another. There were now, besides myself, nine English captives in this place, all of them children, except one woman. I got an opportunity to go and take my leave of them, they being to go one way, and I another. I asked them whether they were earnest with God for deliverance; they told me they did as they were able, and it was some comfort to me that the Lord stirred up children to look to Him. The woman, viz. Goodwife Joslin told me, she shou'd never see me again, and that she could find in her heart to run away. I wisht her not to run away by any means, for we were near thirty miles from any English town, and she very big with child, and had but one week to reckon, and another child in her arms, two years old. And bad rivers there were to go over, & we were feeble with our poor & coarse entertainment. I had my Bible with me; I pulled it out, and asked her whether she would read. We opened the Bible and lighted on Psalm 27, in which Psalm we especially took notice of that verse, viz. "Wait on the Lord, be of good courage, and He shall strengthen thine heart. Wait, I say, on the Lord."

The Fourth Remove

And now I must part with that little company I had. Here I parted from my daughter Mary (whom I never saw again till I saw her in Dorchester, returned from captivity) and from four little cousins and neighbours, some of which I never saw afterward. The Lord only knows the end of them. Amongst them also was that poor woman before mentioned, who came to a sad end, as some of the company told me in my travel. She having much grief upon her spirit about her miserable condition, being so near her time, would be often asking the Indians to let her go home. They not being willing to do that, and yet vexed with her importunity, gathered a great company together about her, and stript her naked, and set her in the midst of them. And when they had sung and danced about her (in their hellish manner) as long as they pleased, they knockt her on head, and the child in her arms with her. When they had done that, they made a fire and put them both into it, and told the other children that were with them, that if they attempted to go home, they would serve them in like manner. The children said she did not shed one tear, but prayed all the while. But to return to my own journey: we travelled about half a day or little more, and came to a desolate place in the wilderness, where there were no wigwams or inhabitants before. We came about the middle of the afternoon to this place, cold and wet, and snowy, and hungry, and weary, and no refreshing for man but the cold ground to sit on and our poor Indian cheer.

Heart-aking thoughts here I had about my poor children, who were scattered up and down among the wild beasts of the forrest. My head was light & dissey (either through hunger or hard lodging,

or trouble, or altogether) my knees feeble, my body raw by sitting double night and day, that I cannot express to man the affliction that lay upon my spirit, but the Lord helped me at that time to express it to Himself. I opened my Bible to read, and the Lord brought that precious scripture to me, Jeremiah 31:16. "Thus saith the Lord, refrain thy voice from weeping, and thine eyes from tears, for thy work shall be rewarded, and they shall come again from the land of the enemy." This was a sweet cordial to me when I was ready to faint. Many and many atime have I sat down and wept sweetly over this scripture. At this place we continued about four dayes.

The Fifth Remove

The occasion (as I thought) of their moving at this time was the English army, it being near and following them, for they went as if they had gone for their lives for some considerable way, and then they made a stop, and chose some of their stoutest men, and sent them back to hold the English army in play whilst the rest escaped. And then, like Jehu, they marched on furiously, with their old, and with their young. Some carried their old decrepit mothers, some carried one, and some another. Four of them carried a great Indian upon a bier, but going through a thick wood with him they were hindred, and could make no haste, whereupon they took him upon their backs, and carried him, one at a time, till they came to Baquag river. Upon a Friday, a little after noon, we came to this river. When all the company was come up, and were gathered together, I thought to count the number of them, but they were so many, and being somewhat in motion, it was beyond my skil. In this travel, because of my wound, I was somewhat favoured in my load. I carried only my knitting work and two quarts of parched meal. Being very faint I asked my mistriss to give me one spoonfull of the meal, but she would not give me a taste. They quickly fell to cutting dry trees, to make rafts to carry them over the river, and soon my turn came to go over. By the advantage of some brush which they had laid upon the raft to sit upon, I did not wet my foot (while many of themselves at the other end were mid-leg deep) which cannot but be acknowledged as a favour of God to my weakened body, it being a very cold time. I was not before acquainted with such kind of doings or dangers. "When thou passest through the water, I will be with thee, and through the rivers, they shall not overflow thee." (Isaiah 43:2) A certain number of us got over the river that night, but it was the night after the Sabbath before all the company was got over. On the Saturday they boyled an old horse's leg (which they had got) and so we drank of the broth as soon as they thought it was ready, and when it was almost gone they filled it up again.

The first week of my being among them, I hardly ate any thing. The second week, I found my stomach grew very faint for want of something, and yet it was very hard to get down their filthy trash, but the third week, though I could think how formerly my stomach would turn against this or that, and I could starve and dy before I could eat such things, yet they were sweet and savory to my taste. I was at this time knitting a pair of white cotton stockins for my mistriss, and had not yet wrought upon a Sabbath day. When the Sabbath came they bade me go to work. I told them it was the Sabbath day and desired them to let me rest, and told them I would do as much more to morrow, to which they answered me, they would break my face.

And here I cannot but take notice of the strange providence of God in preserving the heathen. They were many hundreds, old and young, some sick, and some lame. Many had papooses at their backs; the greatest number at this time with us were squaws, and they travelled with all they had, bag and baggage, and yet they got over this river aforesaid; and on Monday they set their wigwams on fire, and away they went. On that very day came the English army after them to this river, and saw the smoke of their wigwams, and yet this river put a stop to them. God did not give them courage or activity to go over after us. We were not ready for so great a mercy as victory and deliverance. If we had been, God would have found out a way for the English to have passed this river, as well as for the Indians with their squaws and children and all their luggage. "Oh, that my people had hearkened to me, and Israel had walked in my wayes, I should soon have subdued their enemies, and turned my hand against their adversaries," Psalm 81:13,14.

The Sixth Remove

On Monday (as I said) they set their wigwams on fire, and went away. It was a cold morning and before us there was a great brook with ice on it. Some waded through it, up to the knees & higher, but others went until they came to a beaver dam, and I amongst them, where through the good providence of God, I did not wet my foot. I went along that day mourning and lamenting, leaving farther my own country, and travelling into the vast and howling wilderness, and I understood something of Lot's wife's temptation, when she looked back.

We came that day to a great swamp, by the side of which we took up our lodging that night. When I came to the brow of the hill that looked towards the swamp, I thought we had come to a great Indian town (though there were none but our own company). The Indians were as thick as the trees—it seemed as if there had been a thousand hatchets going at once —if one looked before one there was nothing but Indians, and behind one, nothing but Indians, and so on either hand, I myself in the midst, and no Christian soul near me, and yet how hath the Lord preserved me in safety! Oh the experience that I have had of the goodness of God to me and mine!

The Seventh Remove

After a restless and hungry night there, we had a wearisome time of it the next day. The swamp by which we lay was, as it were, a deep dungeon and an exceeding high and steep hill was before it.

Before I got to the top of the hill, I thought my heart and legs, and
all would have broken, and failed me. What through faintness, and
soreness of body, it was a grievous day of travel to me. As wc went
along, I saw a place where English cattle had been. That was
comfort to me, such as it was. Quickly after that we came to an
English path which so took with me, that I thought I could have
freely lyed down and dyed. That day, a little after noon, we came
to Squakeag, where the Indians quickly spread themselves over the
deserted English fields, gleaning what they could find. Some pickt
up ears of wheat that were crickled down, some found ears of Indian
corn, some found ground-nuts, and others sheaves of wheat that
were frozen together in the shock, & went to threshing of them out.
I myself got two ears of Indian corn, and whilst I did but turn my
back, one of them was stolen from me, which much troubled me.
There came an Indian to them at that time with a basket of horse-
liver; I asked him to give me a piece. "What," says he, "can you eat
horse-liver?" I told him I would try if he would give me a piece,
which he did, and I laid it on the coals to roast, but before it was
half ready, they got half of it away from me, so that I was fain to
take the rest and eat it as it was, with the blood about my mouth,
and yet a savory bit it was to me. For the hungry soul every bitter
thing is sweet. A solemn sight methought it was, to see fields of
wheat and Indian corn forsaken and spoiled and the remainders of
them to be food for our merciless enemies. That night we had a
mess of wheat for our supper.

The Eighth Remove

On the morrow morning we must go over the river, i.e.
Connecticut, to meet with King Phillip. Two canoos full they had
carried over; the next turn I myself was to go, but as my foot was
upon the canoo to step in, there was a sudden outcry among them,
and I must step back. And instead of going over the river, I must go
four or five miles up the river farther northward. Some of the
Indians ran one way, and some another. The cause of this rout was,

as I thought, their espying some English scouts who were there-
about. In this travel up the river, about noon, the company made a
stop and sate down, some to eat, and others to rest them.

As I sate amongst them, musing of things past, my son Joseph
unexpectedly came to me. We asked of each other's welfare,
bemoaning our dolcfull condition, and the change that had come
upon us. We had husband, and father, and children, and sisters, and
friends, and relations, and house, and home, and many comforts of
this life, but now we may say, as Job, "Naked I came out of my
mothers womb, and naked shall I return. The Lord gave, and the
Lord hath taken away; blessed be the name of the Lord." I asked
him whether he would read; he told me, he earnestly desired it. I
gave him my Bible, and he lighted upon that comfortable scripture,
Psalm 118:17,18, "I shall not dy, but live, and declare the works of
the Lord. The Lord hath chastened me sore, yet he hath not given
me over to death."

"Look here, mother," says he, "did you read this?" And here I
may take occasion to mention one principal ground of my setting
forth these lines: even as the psalmist sayes, to declare the works
of the Lord, and His wonderfull power in carrying us along,
preserving us in the wilderness, while under the enemies hand, and
returning of us in safety again, and His goodness in bringing to my
hand so many comfortable and suitable scriptures in my distress.

But to return, we travelled on till night, and in the morning,
we must go over the river to Phillip's crew. When I was in the canoo,
I could not but be amazed at the numerous crew of pagans that were
on the bank on the other side. When I came ashore, they gathered
all about me, I sitting alone in the midst. I observed they asked one
another questions, and laughed, and rejoyced over their gains and
victories. Then my heart began to fail and I fell a weeping, which
was the first time to my remembrance that I wept before them.
Although I had met with so much affliction, and my heart was many
times ready to break, yet could I not shed one tear in their sight, but
rather had been all this while in amaze, and like one astonished. But
now I may say as Psalm 137:1, "By the rivers of Babylon, there we
sat down. Yea, we wept when we remembered Zion." There one of
them asked me why I wept: I could hardly tell what to say, yet I
answered, they would kill me. "No," said he, "none will hurt you."
Then came one of them and gave me two spoonfuls of meal to
comfort me, and another gave me half a pint of pease, which was
worth more than many bushels at another time. Then I went to see

King Phillip; he bade me come in and sit down, and asked me whether I would smoke it, (a usual complement now adayes amongst saints and sinners) but this no way suited me. For though I had formerly used tobacco, yet I had left it ever since I was first taken. It seems to be a bait the Devil layes to make men lose their precious time. I remember with shame how, formerly, when I had taken two or three pipes, I was presently ready for another, such a bewitching thing it is. But I thank God, He has now given me power over it. Surely there are many who may be better employed than to ly sucking a stinking tobacco-pipe.

Now the Indians gather their forces to go against North-Hampton. Over-night one went about yelling and hooting to give notice of the design, whereupon they fell to boyling of ground-nuts and parching of corn (as many as had it) for their provision, and in the morning away they went.

During my abode in this place, Phillip spake to me to make a shirt for his boy, which I did, for which he gave me a shilling. I offered the money to my master but he bade me keep it, and with it I bought a piece of horse flesh. Afterwards he asked me to make a cap for his boy, for which he invited me to dinner. I went, and he gave me a pancake, about as big as two fingers. It was made of parched wheat, beaten, and fryed in bear's grease, but I thought I had never tasted pleasanter meat in my life. There was a squaw who spake to me to make a shirt for her sannup, for which she gave me a piece of bear. Another asked me to knit a pair of stockins for which she gave me a quart of pease. I boyled my pease and bear together, and invited my master and mistriss to dinner, but the proud gossip, because I served them both in one dish, would eat nothing, except one bit that he gave her upon the point of his knife.

Hearing that my son was come to this place, I went to see him, and found him lying flat against the ground. I asked him how he could sleep so. He answered me, that he was not asleep, but at prayer, and lay so, that they might not observe what he was doing. I pray God he may remember these things now that he is returned in safety. At this place (the sun now getting higher) what with the beams and heat of the sun and the smoke of the wigwams, I thought I should have been blind, I could scarce discern one wigwam from another. There was here one Mary Thurston of Medfield who seeing how it was with me, lent me a hat to wear, but as soon as I was gone the squaw (who owned that Mary Thurston) came running after me, and got it away again. Here was the squaw that gave me one spoonfull of meal. I put it in my pocket to keep it safe, yet notwithstanding, somebody stole it, but put five Indian corns in the room of it, which corns were the greatest provisions I had in my travel for one day.

The Indians returning from North-Hampton brought with them some horses, and sheep, and other things which they had taken. I desired them, that they would carry me to Albany upon one of those horses, and sell me for powder, for so they had sometimes discoursed. I was utterly hopeless of getting home on foot the way that I came. I could hardly bear to think of the many weary steps I had taken to come to this place.

The Ninth Remove

But in stead of going either to Albany or homeward, we must go five miles up the river and then go over it. Here we abode a while. Here lived a sorry Indian, who spoke to me to make him a shirt, when I had done it, he would pay me nothing. But he, living by the river side, where I often went to fetch water, I would often be putting of him in mind, and calling for my pay. At last he told me if I would make another shirt, for a papoos not yet born, he would give me a knife, which he did when I had done it. I carried the knife in, and my master asked me to give it to him, and I was not a little glad that I had anything that they would accept of, and be pleased with. When we were at this place, my master's maid came home. She had been gone three weeks into the Narrhaganset country, to fetch corn, where they had stored up some in the ground. She brought home about a peck and a half of corn. This was about the time that their great Captain, Naananto, was killed in the Narrhaganset country.

My son being now about a mile from me, I asked liberty to go and see him, they bade me go and away I went, but quickly lost my self, travelling over hills and through swamps, and could not find the way to him. And I cannot but admire the wonderfull power and goodness of God to me, in that, though I was gone from home, and met with all sorts of Indians, and those I had no knowledge of, and

King Phillip

there being no Christian soul near me, yet not one of them offered the least imaginable miscarriage to me. I turned homeward again, and met with my master; he showed me the way to my son. When I came to him I found him not well, and withal he had a boyl on his side, which much troubled him. We bemoaned one another a while, as the Lord helped us, and then I returned again. When I was returned, I found myself as unsatisfied as I was before. I went up and down mourning and lamenting and my spirit was ready to sink with the thoughts of my poor children : my son was ill, and I cound not but think of his mournfull looks, and no Christian friend was near him, to do any office of love for him, either for soul or body. And my poor girl, I knew not where she was, nor whither she was sick, or well, or alive, or dead. I repaired under these thoughts to my Bible (my great comfort in that time) and that scripture came to my hand, "Cast thy burden upon the Lord, and He shall sustain thee." Psalm 55:22.

But I was fain to go and look after something to satisfy my hunger, and going among the wigwams, I went into one and there found a squaw who shewed herself very kind to me, and gave me a piece of bear. I put it into my pocket, and came home, but could not find an opportunity to broil it, for fear they would get it from me, and there it lay all day and night in my stinking pocket. In the morning I went to the same squaw, who had a kettle of ground-nuts boyling. I asked her to let me boyl my piece of bear in her kettle, which she did, and gave me some ground-nuts to eat with it. And I cannot but think how pleasant it was to me. I have sometimes seen bear baked very handsomely among the English, and some liked it, but the thought that it was bear made me tremble. But now that was savory to me that one would think was enough to turn the stomach of a bruit creature.

One bitter cold day, I could find no room to sit down before the fire. I went out and could not tell what to do, but I went in to another wigwam where they were also sitting round the fire. But the squaw laid a skin for me, and bid me sit down, and gave me some ground-nuts, and bade me come again, and told me they would buy me, if they were able, and yet these were strangers to me that I never saw before.

The Tenth Remove

That day a small part of the company removed about three-quarters of a mile, intending further the next day. When they came to the place where they intended to lodge and had pitched their wigwams, being hungry I went again back to the place we were before at, to get something to eat, being encouraged by the squaws kindness, who bade me come again. When I was there, there came an Indian to look after me, who when he had found me, kickt me all along. I went home and found venison roasting that night, but they would not give me one bit of it. Sometimes I met with favour, and sometimes with nothing but frowns.

The Eleventh Remove

The next day in the morning they took their travel intending a dayes journey up the river. I took my load at my back, and quickly we came to wade over the river, and passed some tiresome and wearisome hills. One hill was so steep that I was fain to creep up upon my knees, and to hold by the twiggs and bushes to keep myself from falling backward. My head also was so light that I usually reeled as I went, but I hope all these wearisome steps that I have taken are but a forewarning to me of the heavenly rest. "I know, O Lord, that thy judgements are right, and that Thou in faithfulness hast afflicted me," Psalm 119:75.

The Twelfth Remove

It was upon a Sabbath-day morning that they prepared for their travel. This morning I asked my master whither he would sell me to my husband. He answered me, "Nux," which did much rejoyce my spirit. My mistriss, before we went, was gone to the burial of a papoos, and returning, she found me sitting and reading in my Bible. She snatched it hastily out of my hand, and threw it out of doors. I ran out and catcht it up and put it in my pocket, and never let her see it afterward. They packed up their things to be gone, and gave me my load. I complained it was too heavy, whereupon she gave me a slap in the face, and bade me go; I lifted up my heart to God, hoping that redemption was not far off, and the rather because their insolency grew worse and worse.

But the thoughts of my going homeward (for so we bent our course) much cheered my spirit, and made my burden seem light, and almost nothing at all. But (to my amazement and great perplexity) the scale was soon turned, for when we had gone a little way, on a sudden my mistriss gives out. She would go no further, but turn back again, and said I must go back again with her, and she called her sannup, and would have had him gone back also, but he would not, but said, he would go on, and come back to us again in three dayes. My spirit was upon this, I confess, very impatient, and almost outragious. I thought I could as well have dyed as went back. I cannot declare the trouble that I was in about it, but yet back again I must go. As soon as I had an opportunity, I took my Bible to read, and that quieting scripture came to my hand, Psalm 46:10, "Be still, and know that I am God," which stilled my spirit for the present, but a sore time of tryal, I concluded, I had to go through, my master being gone, who seemed to me the best friend that I had of an Indian, both in cold and hunger, and quickly so it proved. Down I sat, with my heart as full as it could hold, and yet so hungry that I could not sit neither, but going out to see what I could find, and walking

among the trees, I found six acorns, and two ches-nuts, which were
some refreshment to me.

Towards night I gathered me some sticks for my own comfort,
that I might not ly a-cold, but when we came to ly down they bade
me go out, and ly some where else, for they had company (they
said) come in more than their own. I told them, I could not tell where
to go, they bade me go look; I told them, if I went to another
wigwam they would be angry, and send me home again. Then one
of the company drew his sword, and told me he would run me
through if I did not go presently. Then I was fain to stoop to this
rude fellow, and go out in the night, I knew not whither. Mine eyes
have seen that fellow afterwards walking up and down Boston
under the appearance of a friendly Indian, and several others of the
like cut.

I went to one wigwam, and they told me they had no room.
Then I went to another and they said the same. At last an old Indian
bade me come to him, and his squaw gave me some ground-nuts;
she gave me also something to lay under my head, and a good fire
we had. And through the good providence of God, I had a comfortable lodging that night. In the morning another Indian bade me
come at night, and he would give me six ground-nuts, which I did.
We were at this place and time about two miles from the Connecticut river. We went in the morning to gather ground-nuts, to the
river, and went back again that night. I went with a good load at my
back (for they, when they went, though but a little way, would carry
all their trumpery with them) I told them the skin was off my back,
but I had no other comforting answer from them than this, that it
would be no matter if my head were off too.

The Thirteenth Remove

Instead of going toward the bay, which was what I desired, I
must go with them five or six miles down the river into a mighty
thicket of brush, where we abode almost a fortnight. Here one asked
me to make a shirt for her papoos, for which she gave me a mess

of broth which was thickened with meal made of the bark of a tree, and to make it the better, she put into it about a handfull of pease, and a few roasted ground-nuts. I had not seen my son a pritty while, and here was an Indian of whom I made inquiry after him, and asked him when he saw him. He answered me, that such a time his master roasted him, and that himself did eat a piece of him, as big as his two fingers, and that he was very good meat. But the Lord upheld my spirit under this discouragement, and I considered their horrible addictedness to lying, and that there is not one of them that makes the least conscience of speaking of truth.

In this place, on a cold night, as I lay by the fire, I removed a stick that kept the heat from me, a squaw moved it down again, at which I looked up, and she threw a handfull of ashes in mine eyes. I thought I should have been quite blinded, and have never seen more, but lying down, the water ran out of my eyes, and carried the dirt with it, that by the morning, I recovered my sight again. Yet upon this, and the like occasions, I hope it is not too much to say with Job, "Have pity upon me, have pity upon me, O ye my friends, for the hand of the Lord has touched me."

And here I cannot but remember how many times sitting in their wigwams, and musing on things past, I should suddenly leap up and run out, as if I had been at home, forgetting where I was, and what my condition was. But when I was without, and saw nothing but wilderness, and woods, and a company of barbarous heathens, my mind quickly returned to me, which made me think of that, spoken concerning Samson, who said, "I will go out and shake myself as at other times, but he knew not that the Lord was departed from him."

About this time I began to think that all my hopes of restoration would come to nothing. I thought of the English army, and hoped for their coming, and being taken by them, but that failed. I hope to be carried to Albany, as the Indians had discoursed before, but that failed also. I thought of being sold to my husband, as my master spake, but instead of that, my master himself was gone, and I left behind so that my spirit was now quite ready to sink. I asked them to let me go out and pick up some sticks, that I might get alone, and poure out my heart unto the Lord. Then also I took my Bible to read, but I found no comfort here neither, which many times I was wont to find. So easie a thing is it with God to dry up the streames of scripture-comfort from us. Yet I can say that in all my sorrows and afflictions, God did not leave me to have my impatience work

toward Himself, as if His wayes were unrighteous. But I knew that
He laid upon me less than I deserved. Afterward, before this dolefull
time ended with me, I was turning the leaves of my Bible, and the
Lord brought to me some scriptures, which did a little revive me,
as that, Isaiah 55:8, "For My thoughts are not your thoughts, neither
are your wayes My wayes, saith the Lord." And also, that, Psalm
37:5, "Commit thy way unto the Lord, trust also in Him, and He
shall bring it to pass."

About this time they came yelping from Hadley, where they
had killed three English men, and brought one captive with them,
viz., Thomas Read. They all gathered about the poor man, asking
him many questions. I desired also to go and see him; and when I
came, he was crying bitterly, supposing they would quickly kill him.
Whereupon I asked one of them, whether they intended to kill him.
He answered me, they would not. He being a little cheered with
that, I asked him about the welfare of my husband. He told me he
saw him such a time in the bay, and he was well, but very melanchol-
ly, by which I certainly understood (though I suspected it before)
that whatsoever the Indians told me respecting him was vanity and
lies. Some of them told me he was dead, and they had killed him;
some said he was married again, and that the governour wisht him
to marry, and told him he should have his choice, and that were all
perswaded I was dead. So like were these barbarous creatures to
him who was a lyar from the beginning.

As I was sitting once in the wigwams here, Phillip's maid came
in with the child in her arms, and asked me to give her a piece of
my apron to make a flap for it. I told her I would not. Then my
mistriss bade me give it, but still I said no. The maid told me if I
would not give her a piece, she would tear a piece off it. I told her
I would tear her coat. Then with that my mistriss rises up, and takes
up a stick big enough to have killed me, and struck at me with it,
but I stepped out, and she struck the stick into the mat of the
wigwam. But while she was pulling of it out, I ran to the maid and
gave her all my apron, and so that storm went over.

Hearing that my son was come to this place, I went to see him,
and told him his father was well, but very melancholy. He told me
he was as much grieved for his father as for himself. I wondered at
his speech, for I thought I had enough upon my spirit in reference
to my self, to make me mindless of my husband and everyone else,
they being fast among their friends. He told me also, that a while
before, his master (together with other Indians) were going to the

French for powder, but by the way the Mohawks met with them, and killed four of their company which made the rest turn back again, for which I desire that my self and he may bless the Lord, for it might have been worse with him, had he been sold to the French, than it proved to be in his remaining with the Indians.

I went to see an English youth in this place, one John Gilbert of Springfield. I found him lying without doors, upon the ground. I asked him how he did? He told me he was very sick of a flux, with eating so much blood. They had turned him out of the wigwam and with him an Indian papoos, almost dead, (whose parents had been killed) in a bitter cold day, without fire or clothes. The young man himself had nothing on, but his shirt & waistcoat. This sight was enough to melt a heart of flint. There they lay quivering in the cold, the youth round like a dog, the papoos stretcht out, with his eyes and nose and mouth full of dirt, and yet alive, and groaning. I advised John to go and get to some fire. He told me that he could not stand, but I perswaded him still, lest he should ly there and die. And with much adoe I got him to a fire, and went myself home.

As soon as I was got home his master's daughter came after me, to know what I had done with the English man. I told her I had got him to a fire in such a place. Now I need to pray Paul's prayer, 2 Thessalonians 3:2, that we may be delivered from unreasonable and wicked men. For her satisfaction I went along with her, and brought her to him, but before I got home again, it was noised about that I was running away and getting the English youth along with me. As soon as I came in, they began to rant and domineer, asking me where I had been and what I had been doing, and saying that they would knock him on the head. I told them, I had been seeing the English youth, and that I would not run away. They told me I lyed, and taking up a hatchet, they came to me, and said they would knock me down if I stirred out again, and so confined me to the wigwam. Now may I say with David, 2 Samuel 24:14, "I am in a great strait." If I keep in, I must dy with hunger, and if I go out, I must be knockt in head.

This distressed condition held that day, and half the next, and then the Lord remembered me, Whose mercies are great. Then came an Indian to me with a pair of stockins that were too big for him, and he would have me ravel them out, and knit them fit for him. I shewed my self willing, and bid him ask my mistriss if I might go along with him a little way. She said yes, I might, but I was not a little refresht with that news, that I had my liberty again. Then I went along with him, and he gave me some roasted ground-nuts, which did again revive my feeble stomach.

Being got out of her sight, I had time and liberty again to look into my Bible, which was my guide by day, and my pillow by night. Now that comfortable scripture presented itself to me, Isaiah 54:7. "For a small moment have I forsaken thee, but with great mercies will I gather thee." Thus the Lord carried me along from one time to another, and made good to me this precious promise, and many others. Then my son came to see me, and I asked his master to let him stay a while with me, that I might comb his head, and look over him, for he was almost over come with lice. He told me, when I had done, that he was very hungry, but I had nothing to relieve him, but bid him to go into the wigwams as he went along, and see if he could get anything among them, which he did, and it seemes tarried a little too long, for his master was angry with him, and beat him, and then sold him. Then he came running to tell me he had a new master, and that he had given him some ground-nuts already. Then I went along with him to his new master who told me he loved him, and he should not want. So his master carried him away and I never saw him afterward, till I saw him at Pascataqua in Portsmouth.

That night they bade me go out of the wigwam again. My mistresses papoos was sick, and it died that night, and there was one benefit in it, that there was more room. I went to a wigwam and they bade me come in, and gave me a skin to ly upon, and a mess of venison and ground-nuts, which was a choice dish among them. On the morrow they buried the papoos, and afterward, both morning and evening, there came a company to mourn and howle with her, though I confess, I could not much console with them. Many sorrowfull dayes I had in this place, often getting alone, "Like a crane, or a swallow, so did I chatter; I did mourn as a dove, mine eyes fail with looking upward. O Lord, I am oppressed, undertake for me." Isaiah 38:14. I could tell the Lord, as Hezekiah, verse 3. "Remember now O Lord, I beseech Thee, how I have walked before Thee in truth."

Now had I time to examine all my wayes. My conscience did not accuse me of un-righteousness toward one or another, yet I saw how in my walk with God, I had been a careless creature. As David said, "Against Thee, Thee only have I sinned," & I might say with the poor publican, "God be mercifull unto me, a sinner." On the Sabbath-dayes I could look upon the sun and think how people were going to the house of God, to have their souls refresht, & then home, and their bodies also. But I was destitute of both, & and might say as the poor prodigal, "He would fain have filled his belly with the husks that the swine did eat, and no man gave unto him," Luke 15:16. For I must say with him, "Father I have sinned against heaven and in thy sight," verse 21. I remembered how on the night before & after the Sabbath, when my family was about me, and relations and neighbours with us, we could pray and sing, and then refresh our bodies with the good creatures of God, and then have a comfortable bed to ly down on. But in stead of all this, I had only a little swill for the body, and then like a swine, must ly down on the ground. I cannot express to man the sorrow that lay upon my spirit. The Lord knows it. Yet that comfortable scripture would often come to my mind, "For a small moment have I forsaken thee, but with great mercies will I gather thee."

The Fourteenth Remove

Now must we pack up and be gone from this thicket, bending our course toward the bay-towns, I having nothing to eat by the way this day, but a few crumbs of cake, that an Indian gave my girl the same day we were taken. She gave it to me, and I put it in my pocket. There it lay till it was so mouldy (for want of good baking) that one could not tell what it was made of; it fell all to crumbs & grew so dry and hard that it was like little flints. And this refreshed me many times, when I was ready to faint. It was in my thoughts when I put it into my mouth, that if ever I returned, I would tell the world what a blessing the Lord gave to such mean food. As we went along, they killed a deer with a young one in her. They gave me a piece of the fawn, and it was so young and tender that one might eat the bones as well as the flesh, and yet I thought it very good. When night came on we sate down; it rained, but they quickly got up a bark wigwam, where I lay dry that night. I looked out in the morning, and many of them had line in the rain all night, I saw by their reaking. Thus the Lord dealt mercifully with me many times and I fared better than many of them. In the morning they took the blood of the deer,

and put it into the paunch, and so boyled it. I could eat nothing of
that, though they ate it sweetly. And yet they were so nice in other
things, that when I had fetcht water and had put the dish I dipt the
water with into the kettle of water which I brought, they would say,
they would knock me down, for they said it was a sluttish trick.

The Fifteenth Remove

We went on our travel. I, having got one handfull of ground-
nuts for my support that day they, gave me my load and I went on
cheerfully (with the thoughts of going homeward) having my
burden more on my back than my spirit. We came to Baquag river
again that day, near which we abode a few dayes. Sometimes one
of them would give me a pipe, another a little tobacco, another a
little salt, which I would change for a little victuals. I cannot but
think what a wolvish appetite persons have in a starving condition,
for many times when they gave me that which was hot, I was so
greedy that I should burn my mouth, that it would trouble me hours
after, and yet I should quickly do the same again. And after I was
thoroughly hungry, I was never again satisfied. For though sometimes it fell out that I got enough, and did eat till I could eat no more,
yet I was as unsatisfied as I was when I began. And now I could see
that scripture verified, (there being many scriptures which we do
not take notice of, or understand till we are afflicted) Micah 4:14.
"Thou shalt eat and not be satisfied." Now might I see more than
ever before, the miseries that sin hath brought upon us. Many times
I should be ready to run out against the heathen, but the scripture
would quiet me again, Amos 3:6, "Shall there be evil in the city,
and the Lord hath not done it?" The Lord help me to make a right
improvement of His word, and that I might learn that great lesson,
Micah 6:8,9. "He hath shewed thee (oh man) what is good, and what
doth the Lord require of thee, but to do justly, and love mercy, and
walk humbly with thy God? Hear ye the rod, and who hath ap-
pointed it."

The Sixteenth Remove

We began this remove with wading over Baquag river. The water was up to the knees, and the stream very swift, and so cold that I thought it would have cut me in sunder. I was so weak and feeble, that I reeled as I went along and thought there I must end my dayes at last, after my bearing and getting thorough so many difficulties. The Indians stood laughing to see me staggering along, but in my distress the Lord gave me experience of the truth, and goodness of that promise, Isaiah 43:2. "When thou passest thorough the waters, I will be with thee, and through the rivers, they shall not overflow thee." Then I sat down to put on my stockins and shoes, with the tears running down mine eyes, and many sorrowfull thoughts in my heart, but I gat up to go along with them.

Quickly there came up to us an Indian, who informed them, that I must go to Wachusett to my master, for there was a letter come from the Council to the Saggamores about redeeming the captives, and that there would be another in fourteen dayes, and that I must be there ready. My heart was so heavy before that I could scarce speak or go in the path, and yet now so light, that I could run. My strength seemed to come again, and recruit my feeble knees, and aking heart. Yet it pleased them to go but one mile that night, and there we stayed two dayes. In that time came a company of Indians to us, near thirty, all on horse-back. My heart skipt within me, thinking they had been English men at the first sight of them, for they were dressed in English apparel, with hats, white neckcloths, and sashes about their waists, and ribbonds upon their shoulders. But when they came near, there was a vast difference between the lovely faces of Christians, and the foul looks of those heathens, which much damped my spirit again.

The Seventeenth Remove

A comfortable remove it was to me, because of my hopes. They gave me a pack, and along we went cheerfully, but quickly my will proved more than my strength. Having little or no refreshing, my strength failed me, and my spirit was almost quite gone. Now may I say with David, Psalm 109:22-24, "I am poor and needy, and my heart is wounded within me. I am gone like the shadow when it declineth; I am tossed up and down like the locust. My knees are weak through fasting, and my flesh faileth of fatness." At night we came to an Indian town, and the Indians sate down by a wigwam, discoursing, but I was almost spent, and could scarce speak. I laid down my load, and went into the wigwam, and there sat an Indian boyling horse's feet (they being wont to eat the flesh first, and when the feet were old and dried, and they had nothing else, they would cut off the feet and use them). I asked him to give me a little of his broth, or water they were boyling in. He took a dish and gave me one spoonfull of samp, and bid me take as much of the broth as I would. Then I put some of the hot water to the samp, and drank it up, and my spirit came again. He gave me also a piece of the ruff or ridding of the small guts, and I broiled it on the coals, and now may I say with Jonathan, "See, I pray you, how mine eyes have been enlightened, because I tasted a little of this honey," 1 Samuel 14:29. Now is my spirit revived again. Though means be never so inconsiderable, yet if the Lord bestow His blessing upon them, they shall refresh both soul and body.

The Eighteenth Remove

We took up our packs and along we went, but a wearisome day I had of it. As we went along I saw an English- man stript naked, and lying dead upon the ground, but knew not who it was. Then we came to another Indian town, where we stayed all night. In this town there were four English children, captives, and one of them my own sister's. I went to see how she did, and she was well, considering her captive-condition. I would have tarried that night with her, but they that owned her would not suffer it. Then I went into another wigwam, where they were boyling corn and beans, which was a lovely sight to see, but I could not get a taste thereof. Then I went to another wigwam, where there were two of the English children. The squaw was boyling horse's feet; then she cut me off a little piece, and gave one of the English children a piece also. Being very hungry I had quickly eaten up mine, but the child could not bite it, it was so tough and sinewy, but lay sucking, gnawing, chewing and slabbering of it in the mouth and hand. Then I took it of the child and ate it my self, and savory it was to my taste. Then I may say as Job, Chapter 6:7, "The things that my soul refused to touch, are as my sorrowfull meat." Thus the Lord made that pleasant and refreshing, which another time would have been an abomination. Then I went home to my mistresses wigwam, and they told me I disgraced my master with begging, and if I did so any more, they would knock me in the head. I told them they had as good knock me in the head as starve me to death.

The Nineteenth Remove

They said when we went out, that we must travel to Wachusett this day. But a bitter weary day I had of it, travelling now three dayes together without resting any day between. At last, after many weary steps, I saw Wachusett hills, but many miles off. Then we came to a great swamp, through which we travelled up to the knees, in mud and water, which was heavy going to one tyred before. Being almost spent, I thought I should have sunk down at last, and never gat out; but I may say, as in Psalm 94:18, "When my foot slipped, Thy mercy, O Lord helped me up." Going along, having indeed my life, but little spirit, Phillip, who was in the company, came up and took me by the hand and said, "Two weeks more and you shall be mistriss again." I asked him if he spake true? He answered, "Yes, and quickly you shall come to your master again," who had been gone from us three weeks. After many weary steps we came to Wachusett where he was, and glad I was to see him. He asked me, when I washt me? I told him not this month; then he fetcht me some water himself, and bid me wash, and gave me the glass to see how I lookt and bid his squaw give me something to eat. So she gave me a mess of beans and meat, and a little ground-nut cake. I was wonderfully revived with this favor shewed me. Psalm 106:46, "He made them also to be pitied, of all those that carried them captives."

My master had three squaws, living sometimes with one, and sometimes with another one. This old squaw, at whose wigwam I was, and with whom my master had been those three weeks. Another was Weetamoo, with whom I had lived and served all this while, a severe and proud dame she was, bestowing every day in dressing herself neat as much time as any of the gentry of the land, powdering her hair, and painting her face, going with neck-laces, with jewels in her ears, and bracelets upon her hands. When she had dressed herself, her work was to make girdles of wampum and beads. The third squaw was a younger one, by whom he had two papooses.

By the time I was refreshed by the old squaw, with whom my master was, Weetamoo's maid came to call me home, at which I fell a weeping. Then the old squaw told me, to encourage me, that if I wanted victuals, I should come to her, and that I should ly there in her wigwam. Then I went with the maid, and quickly came again and lodged there. The squaw laid a mat under me, and a good rugg over me—the first time I had any such kindness shewed me. I understood that Weetamoo thought that if she should let me go and serve with the old squaw, she would be in danger to lose, not only my service, but the redemption-pay also. And I was not a little glad to hear this, being by it raised in my hopes that in God's due time there would be an end of this sorrowfull hour. Then came an Indian and asked me to knit him three pairs of stockins for which I had a hat and a silk handkerchief. Then another asked me to make her a shirt, for which she gave me an apron.

Then came Tom and Peter with the second letter from the Council about the captives. Though they were Indians, I gat them by the hand, and burst out into tears—my heart was so full that I could not speak to them—but recovering myself, I asked them how my husband did, & all my friends and acquaintances? They said they are all very well, but melancholy. They brought me two biskets, and a pound of tobacco. The tobacco I quickly gave away. When it was all gone, one asked me to give him a pipe of tobacco. I told him it was all gone; then he began to rant and threaten. I told him when my husband came I would give him some. "Hang him, rogue," says he, "I will knock out his brains, if he comes here." And then again, in the same breath they would say that if there should come a hundred without guns, they would do them no hurt. So unstable and like mad men they were. So that, fearing the worst, I durst not send to my husband, though there were some thoughts of his coming to redeem and fetch me, not knowing what might follow, for there was little more trust to them than to the master they served. When the letter was come, the Saggamores met to consult about the captives, and called me to them to enquire how much my husband would give to redeem me. When I came I sate down among them, as I was wont to do, as their manner is. They bade me stand up, and said they were the general court. They bid me speak what I thought he would give. Now knowing that all we had was destroyed by the Indians, I was in a great strait. I thought if I should speak but a little, it would be slighted, and hinder the matter; if of a great sum, I knew not where it would be procured. Yet at a venture, I said twenty pounds, yet desired them to take less, but they would not hear of that, but sent that message to Boston, that for twenty pounds I should be redeemed. It was a praying Indian that wrote their letter for them.

There was another praying Indian who told me that he had a brother that would not eat horse, his conscience was so tender and scrupulous (though large as hell, for the destruction of poor Christians). Then, he said, he read that scripture to him, 2 Kings, 6:25, "There was a famine in Samaria, and behold they besieged it, until an asses head was sold for fourscore pieces of silver, and the fourth part of a kab of doves dung, for five pieces of silver." He expounded this place to his brother, and shewed him that it was lawfull to eat that in a famine which is not at another time. And now, sayes he, he will eat horse with any Indian of them all.

There was another praying Indian who, when he had done all the mischief that he could, betrayed his own father into the English hands, thereby to purchase his own life. Another praying Indian was at Sudbury-fight, though, as he deserved, he was afterwards hanged for it. There was another praying Indian, so wicked and cruel as to wear a string about his neck, strung with Christian's fingers. Another praying Indian, when they went to Sudbury-fight, went with them, and his squaw also with him, with her papoos at her back. Before they went to that fight, they got a company together to powaw. The manner was as followeth:

There was one that kneeled upon a deer-skin, with the company round him in a ring who kneeled, and striking upon the ground with their hands, and with sticks, and muttering or humming with their mouths. Besides him who kneeled in the ring, there also stood one with a gun in his hand. Then he on the deer-skin made a speech, and all manifested assent to it, and so they did many times together. Then they bade him with the gun go out of the ring, which he did, but when he was out, they called him in again. But he seemed to make a stand; then they called the more earnestly, till he returned again; then they all sang. Then they gave him two guns, in either hand, one. And so he on the deer-skin began again, and at the end of every sentence in his speaking, they all assented, humming or muttering with their mouths, and striking upon the ground with their hands. Then they bade him with the two guns go out of the ring again, which he did, a little way. Then they called him in again, but he made a stand. So they called him with greater earnestness, but he stood reeling and wavering as if he knew not whither he should stand or fall, or which way to go. Then they called him with

exceeding great vehemency, all of them, one and another. After a little while he turned in, staggering as he went, with his arms stretcht out, in either hand a gun. As soon as he came in, they all sung and rejoyced exceedingly a while. And then he upon the deer-skin made another speech unto which they all assented in a rejoycing manner. And so they ended their business, and forthwith went to Sudbury fight.

To my thinking they went without any scruple, but that they should prosper and gain the victory, and they went out not so rejoycing, but they came home with as great a victory. For they said they had killed two captains, and almost a hundred men. One English-man they brought along with them, and he said it was too true, for they had made sad work at Sudbury, as indeed it proved. Yet they came home without that rejoycing and triumphing over their victory which they were wont to shew at other times, but rather like dogs (as they say) which have lost their ears. Yet I could not perceive that it was for their own loss of men. They said, they had not lost above five or six, and I missed none, except in one wigwam. When they went, they acted as if the devil had told them they should have a fall. Whither it were so or no, I cannot tell, but so it proved, for quickly they began to fall, and so held on that summer, till they came to utter ruine. They came home on a Sabbath day, and the powaw that kneeled upon the deer-skin came home (I may say without abuse) as black as the devil.

When my master came home, he came to me and bid me make a shirt for his papoos, of a Holland laced pillowbeer. About that time there came an Indian to me and bid me come to his wigwam, at night and he would give me some pork & ground- nuts, which I did. And as I was eating, another Indian said to me, he seems to be your good friend, but he killed two Englishmen at Sudbury, and there ly their cloaths behind you. I looked behind me, and there I saw bloody cloaths, with bullet holes in them. Yet the Lord suffered not this wretch to do me any hurt. Yea, instead of that, he many times refresht me: five or six times did he and his squaw refresh my feeble carcass. If I went to their wigwam at any time they would alwayes give me something, and yet they were strangers that I never saw before. Another squaw gave me a piece of fresh pork, and a little salt with it, and lent me her pan to fry it in, and I cannot but remember what a sweet, pleasant and delightfull relish that bit had to me, to this day. So little do we prize common mercies when we have them to the full.

The Twentieth Remove

It was their usual manner to remove, when they had done any mischief, lest they should be found out, and so they did at this time. We went about three or four miles and there they built a great wigwam, big enough to hold a hundred Indians, which they did in preparation to a great day of dancing. They would say now amongst themselves that the Governour would be so angry for his loss at Sudbury, that they would send no more about the captives, which made me grieve and tremble. My sister, being not far from the place where we now were, and hearing that I was here, desired her master to let her come and see me, and he was willing to it, and would go with her. But she being ready before him, told him she would go before, and was come within a mile or two of the place. Then he overtook her, and began to rant as if he had been mad, and made her go back again in the rain, so that I never saw her till I saw her in Charlestown. But the Lord requited many of their ill doings. For this Indian, her master, was hanged afterward at Boston. The Indians now began to come from all quarters, against their merry dancing day. Among some of them came one Goodwife Kettle. I told her my heart was so heavy that it was ready to break. "So is mine too," said she, but yet said, "I hope we shall hear some good news shortly." I could hear how earnestly my sister desired to see me, & I as earnestly desired to see her, and yet neither of us could get an opportunity. My daughter was also now about a mile off, and I had not seen her in nine or ten weeks, as I had not seen my sister since our first taking. I earnestly desired them to let me go and see them. Yea, I intreated, begged, and perswaded them but to let me see my daughter, and yet so hard hearted were they, that they would not suffer it. They made use of their tyrranical power whilst they had it. But through the Lord's wonderfull mercy, their time was now but short.

On a Sabbath-day, the sun being about an hour high in the afternoon, came Mr. John Hoar (the Council permitting him, and his own forward spirit inclining him) together with the two afore mentioned Indians, Tom and Peter, with their third letter from the council. When they came near, I was abroad. Though I saw them not, they presently called me in, and bade me sit down and not stir. Then they catcht up their guns, and away they ran, as if an enemy had been at hand, and the guns went off apace. I manifested some great trouble, and they asked me what was the matter? I told them I thought they had killed the English-man (for they had in the meantime informed me that an English-man was come). They said no. They shot over his horse, and under, and before his horse, and they pusht him this way and that way, at their pleasure, shewing what they could do. Then they let them come to their wigwams. I begged of them to let me see the English man, but they would not. But there was I fain to sit their pleasure. When they had talked their fill with him, they suffered me to go to him. We asked each other of our welfare, and how my husband did, and all my friends. He told me they were all well, and would be glad to see me. Amongst other things which my husband sent me, there came a pound of tobacco which I sold for nine shillings in money. For many of the Indians, for want of tobacco, smoked hemlock and ground-ivy. It was a great mistake in any, who thought I sent for tobacco, for through the favour of God, that desire was overcome. I now asked them, whither I should go home with Mr. Hoar? They answered no, one and another of them, and it being night we laid down with that answer.

In the morning, Mr. Hoar invited the Saggamores to dinner, but when we went to get it ready, we found they had stolen the greatest part of the provision Mr. Hoar had brought, out of his bags, in the night. And we may see the wonderfull power of God, in that one passage, in that when there was such a great number of Indians together, and so greedy of a little good food, and no English there, but Mr. Hoar and myself, that there they did not knock us in the head and take what we had, there being not only some provisions, but trading-cloth and a part of the twenty pounds agreed upon. But instead of doing us any mischief they seemed to be ashamed of the fact, and said, it were some Machit Indians that did it. Oh, that we could believe that there is nothing too hard for God! God shewed His power over the heathen in this, as He did over the hungry lyons when Daniel was cast into the den. Mr. Hoar called them betime to dinner, but they ate very little, they being so busy in dressing themselves, and getting ready for their dance, which was carried on by eight of them; four men and four squaws, my master and mistriss being two.

He was dressed in his Holland shirt with great laces sewed at the tail of it. He had his silver buttons, and his white stockins. His garters were hung round with shillings, and he had girdles of wampum upon his head and shoulders. She had a Kersey coat, and was covered with girdles of wampum from the loins upward. Her arms from her elbows to her hands were covered with bracelets; there were handfuls of neck laces about her neck, and several sorts of jewels in her ears. She had fine red stockins, and white shoes, her hair powdered and face painted red, that was always before black. And all the dancers were after the same manner. There were two others singing and knocking on a kettle for their musick. They kept hopping up and down one after another, with a kettle of water in the midst, standing warm upon some embers, to drink of when they were dry. They held on till it was almost night, throwing out wampum to the standers by. At night I asked them again if I should go home? They all as one said no, except my husband would come for me.

When we were lain down, my master went out of the wigwam, and by and by sent in an Indian called James the Printer, who told Mr. Hoar, that my master would let me go to morrow, if he would let him have one pint of liquors. Then Mr. Hoar called his own Indians, Tom and Peter, and bid them go and see whither he would promise it before them three, and if he would, he should have it, which he did, and he had it. Then Phillip, smelling the business called me to him, and asked me what I would give him, to tell me some good news, and speak a good word for me. I told him, I could not tell what to give him, I would anything I had, and asked him what he would have? He said two coats and twenty shillings in money, and half a bushel of feed corn, and some tobacco. I thanked him for his love, but I knew the good news as well as the crafty fox. My master after he had his drink, quickly came ranting into the wigwam again, and called for Mr. Hoar, drinking to him, and saying he was a good man, and then again he would say, "Hang him, rogue." Being almost drunk, he would drink to him, and yet presently say he should be hanged. Then he called for me, I trembled to hear him, yet I was fain to go to him, and he drank to me, shewing no incivility. He was the first Indian I saw drunk all the while that I was amongst them. At last his squaw ran out, and he after her, round the wigwam, with his money jingling at his knees, but she escaped him. But having an old squaw he ran to her, and lo through the Lord's mercy, we were no more troubled that night.

Yet I had not a comfortable night's rest, for I think I can say, I did not sleep for three nights together. The night before the letter came from the Council, I could not rest, I was so full of fears and troubles, God many times leaving us most in the dark, when deliverance is nearest. Yea, at this time I could not rest night nor day. The next night I was overjoyed, Mr. Hoar being come, and that with such good tidings. This third night I was even swallowed up with thoughts of things, viz., that ever I should go home again, and that I must go, leaving my children behind me in the wilderness, so that sleep was now almost departed from mine eyes.

On Tuesday morning they called their General Court (as they call it) to consult and determine whether I should go home or no, and they all as one man did seemingly consent to it, that I should go home, except Phillip, who would not come among them.

But before I go any further, I would take leave to mention a few remarkable passages of providence, which I took special notice of in my afflicted time:

1. Of the fair opportunity lost in the long march a little after the fort-fight, when our English army was so numerous, and in pursuit of the enemy, and so near as to take several and destroy them, and the enemy in such distress for food, that our men might track them by their rooting in the earth for ground-nuts whilst they were flying for their lives. I say that then our army should want provision, and be forced to leave their pursuit and return homeward, and the very next week the enemy came upon our town, like bears bereft of their whelps, or so many ravenous wolves, rending us and our lambs to death. But what shall I say? God seemed to leave His people to themselves, and order all things for His own holy ends. Shall there be evil in the city and the Lord hath not done it? They are not grieved for the affliction of Joseph, therefore shall they go captive with the first that go captive. It is the Lord's doing, and it should be marvelous in our eyes.

2. I cannot but remember how the Indians derided the slowness, and dullness of the English army, in its setting out. For after the desolations at Lancaster and Medfield, as I went along with them, they asked me when I thought the English army would come after them? I told them I could not tell. "It may be they will come

in May," said they. Thus did they scoff at us, as if the English would be a quarter of a year getting ready.

3. Which also I have hinted before, when the English army with new supplies were sent forth to pursue after the enemy, & they understanding it, fled before them till they came to Baquag river, where they forthwith went over safely, that that river should be impassable to the English. I can but admire to see the wonderfull providence of God in preserving the heathen for farther affliction to our poor country. They could go in great numbers over, but the English must stop. God had an over-ruling hand in all those things.

4. It was thought, if the corn were cut down, they would starve and dy with hunger, and all their corn that could be found was destroyed, and they driven from that little they had in store, into the woods in the midst of winter. And yet how to admiration did the Lord preserve them for His holy ends, and the destruction of many still amongst the English! Strangely did the Lord provide for them, that I did not see (all the time I was among them) one man, woman, or child, dy with hunger.

Though many times they would eat that, that a hog or a dog would hardly touch, yet by that, God strengthened them to be a scourge to His people.

The chief and commonest food was ground-nuts. They eat also nuts and acorns, harty choakes, lilly roots, ground- beans, and several other weeds and roots, that I know not. They would pick up old bones, and cut them to pieces at the joynts, and if they were full of wormes and magots, they would scald them over the fire to make the vermine come out, and then boyl them, and drink up the liquor, and then beat the great ends of them in a mortar, and so eat them. They would eat horses guts, and ears, and all sorts of wild birds which they would catch—also bear, venison, beaver, tortois, frogs, squirrels, dogs, skunks, rattle-snakes, yea, the very bark of trees, besides all sorts of creatures, and provision which they plundered from the English. I can but stand in admiration to see the wonderfull power of God, in providing for such a vast number of our enemies in the wilderness where there was nothing to be seen, but from hand to mouth. Many times in a morning, the generality of them would eat up all they had, and yet have some farther supply against what they wanted. It is said, Psalm 81:13,14, "Oh that my people had hearkened to me, and Israel had walked in my wayes, I should soon have subdued their enemies, and turned my hand against their adversaries." But now our perverse and evil carriages in the sight of the Lord have so offended Him, that instead of turning His hand against them, the Lord feeds & nourishes them up to be a scourge to the whole land.

5. Another thing that I would observe is the strange providence of God in turning things about when the Indians were at the highest, and the English at the lowest. I was with the enemy eleven weeks and five dayes, and not one week passed without the fury of the enemy, and some desolation by fire and sword upon one place or other. They mourned (with their black faces) for their own losses, yet triumphed and rejoyced in their inhumane, and many times devilish cruelty to the English. They would boast much of their victories, saying that in two hours time they had destroyed such a captain and his company at such a place, and such a captain and his company in such a place, and such a captain and his company in such a place, and boast how many towns they had destroyed, and then scoff, and say they had done them a good turn to send them to heaven so soon. Again they would say, this summer that they would knock all the rogues in the head, or drive them into the sea, or make them flee the country, thinking surely, Agag-like, the bitterness of death is past.

Now the heathen begin to think all is their own, & the poor Christian's hopes to fail (as to man) and now their eyes are more to God, and their hearts sigh heaven-ward, and to say in good earnest, "Help Lord, or we perish." When the Lord had brought His people to this, that they saw no help in anything but Himself, then He takes the quarrel into His own hand, and though they had made a pit, in their own imaginations, as deep as hell for the Christians that summer, yet the Lord hurll'd them into it. And the Lord had not so many wayes before to preserve them, but now He hath as many to destroy them.

But to return again to my going home, where we may see a remarkable change of providence: At first they were all against it, except my husband would come for me, but afterwards they assented to it, and seemed much to rejoyce in it. Some asked me to send them some bread, others some tobacco, others shaking me by the hand, offering me a hood and scarfe to ride in, not one moving hand or tongue against it. Thus hath the Lord answered my poor desire, and the many earnest requests of others put up unto God for me.

In my travels an Indian came to me and told me, if I were willing, he and his squaw would run away and go home along with me. I told him no. I was not willing to run away, but desired to wait God's time, that I might go home quietly, and without fear. And now God hath granted me my desire.

O the wonderfull power of God that I have seen, and the experience that I have had! I have been in the midst of those roaring lyons, and salvage bears, that feared neither God, nor man, nor the devil, by night and day, alone and in company, sleeping all sorts together. And yet not one of them ever offered me the least abuse of unchastity to me, in word or action. Though some are ready to say I speak this for my own credit, I speak it in the presence of God, and to His glory. God's power is as great now, and as sufficient to save, as when He preserved Daniel in the lyons den, or the three children in the firey furnace. I may well say as His Psalm 107:12, "Oh give thanks unto the Lord for He is good, for His mercy endureth for ever. Let the redeemed of the Lord say so, whom He hath redeemed from the hand of the enemy," especially that I should have come away in the midst of so many hundreds of enemies quietly and peacefully, and not a dog moving his tongue.

So I took my leave of them, and in coming along my heart melted into tears, more than all the while I was with them, and I was almost swallowed up with the thoughts that ever I should go home again. About the sun going down, Mr. Hoar and myself and the two Indians came to Lancaster, and a solemn sight it was to me. There had I lived many comfortable years amongst my relations and neighbours, and now not one Christian was to be seen, nor one house left standing. We went on to a farm-house that was yet standing, where we lay all night, and a comfortable lodging we had, though there was nothing but straw to ly on. The Lord preserved us in safety that night, and raised us up again in the morning, and carried us along, that before noon we came to Concord. Now I was full of joy, and yet not without sorrow: joy to see such a lovely sight, so many Christians together, and some of my neighbours. There I met with my brother, and my brother in law, who asked me if I knew where his wife was. Poor heart! He had helped to bury her, and knew it not. She being shot down by the house was partly burnt, so that those who were at Boston at the desolation of the town and came back afterward and buried the dead did not know her. Yet I was not without sorrow, to think how many were looking and longing, and my own children among the rest, to enjoy that deliverance that I had now received. And I did not know whither ever I should see them again.

Being recruited with food and raiment, we went to Boston that day, where I met with my dear husband, but the thoughts of our dear children, one being dead, and the other we could not tell where, abated our comfort each to other. I was not before so much hem'd in with the merciless and cruel heathen, but now as much with pitiful, tender-hearted, and compassionate Christians. In that poor and distressed and beggarly condition I was received in, I was kindly entertained in several houses. So much love I received from several (some of whom I knew, and others I knew not) that I am not capable to declare it. But the Lord knows them all by name. The Lord reward them seven fold into their bosoms of His spirituals for their temporals. The twenty pounds, the price of my redemption, was raised by some Boston gentlemen, and Mr. Usher, whose bounty and religious charity, I would not forget to make mention of. Then Mr. Thomas Shepard of Charlestown received us into his house where we continued eleven weeks. And a father and mother they were to us. And many more tender-hearted friends we met with in that place. We were now in the midst of love, yet not without much and frequent heaviness of heart for our poor children, and other relations, who were still in affliction.

The week following, after my coming in, the Governour and Council sent forth to the Indians again, and that not without success, for they brought in my sister, and Good-wife Kettle. Their not knowing where our children were was a sore tryal to us still, and yet we were not without secret hopes that we should see them again. That which was dead lay heavier upon my spirit than those which were live and amongst the heathen; thinking how it suffered with its wounds, and I was no way able to relieve it, and how it was buried by the heathen in the wilderness from among all Christians. We were hurried up and down in our thoughts, sometime we should hear a report that they were gone this way, and sometimes that, and that they were come in in this place or that. We kept enquiring and listning to hear concerning them, but no certain news as yet.

About this time the Council had ordered a day of publick thanks-giving. Though I thought I had still cause of mourning, and being unsettled in our minds, we thought we would ride toward the eastward, to see if we could hear anything concerning our children. And as we were riding along (God is the wise disposer of all things) between Ipswich and Rowly, we met with Mr. William Hubbard, who told us that our son Joseph was come in to Major Waldron's, and another with him, which was my sister's son. I asked him how he knew it? He said the Major himself told him so. So along we went till we came to Newbury, and their minister being absent, they desired my husband to preach the thanks-giving for them, but he was not willing to stay there that night, but would go over to Salisbury, to hear further and come again in the morning, which he did, and preached there that day.

At night, when he had done, one came and told him that his daughter was come in at Providence. Here was mercy on both hands. Now hath God fulfilled that precious scripture which was such a comfort to me in my distressed condition. When my heart was ready to sink into the earth (my children being gone I could not tell whither) and my knees trembled under me, and I was walking through the valley of the shadow of death, then the Lord brought, and now has fulfilled, that reviving word unto me: "Thus saith the Lord, refrain thy voice from weeping, and thine eyes from tears, for thy work shall be rewarded, saith the Lord, and they shall come again from the land of the enemy." Now were we between them, the one on the east, and the other on the west. Our son being nearest, we went to him first, to Portsmouth, where we met with him, and with the Major also, who told us he had done what he could, but could not redeem him under seven pounds, which the good people thereabouts were pleased to pay. The Lord reward the Major, and all the rest, though unknown to me, for their labor of love. My sister's son was redeemed for four pounds, which the council gave order for the payment of. Having now received one of our children, we hastened toward the other. Going back through Newbury, my husband preached there on the Sabbath-day, for which they rewarded him many fold.

On Monday we came to Charlestown, were we learned that the Governour of Road-Island had sent over for our daughter, to take care of her, being now within his jurisdiction, which should not pass without our acknowledgements. But being nearer Rehoboth than Road-Island, Mr. Newman went over, and took care of her, and brought her to his own house. And the goodness of God was admirable to us in our low estate, in that He raised up passionate friends on every side to us, when we had nothing to recompense any for their love.

The Indians were now gone that way and it was apprehended dangerous to go to her, but the carts which carried provision to the English army, being guarded, brought her with them to Dorchester, where we received her safe. Blessed be the Lord for it, for great is His power, and He can do whatsoever seemeth Him good.

Her coming in was after this manner: she was travelling one day with the Indians, with her basket at her back. The company of Indians were got before her, and gone out of sight, all except one squaw. She followed the squaw till night, and then both of them lay down, having nothing over them but the heavens, and under them but the earth. Thus she travelled three dayes together, not knowing whither she was going, having nothing to eat or drink but water and green hortle-berries. At last they came into Providence, where she was kindly entertained by several of that town.

The Indians often said that I should never have her under twenty pounds, but now the Lord hath brought her in upon free cost, and given her to me the second time. The Lord make us a blessing indeed, each to others. Now have I seen that scripture also fulfilled, Deuteronomy 30:4,7, "If any of thine be driven out to the outmost parts of heaven, from thence will the Lord thy God gather thee, and from thence will He fetch thee. And the Lord thy God will put all these curses upon thine enemies, and on them which hate thee, which persecuted thee." Thus hath the Lord brought me and mine out of that horrible pit and hath set us in the midst of tender- hearted and compassionate Christians. It is the desire of my soul, that we may walk worthy of the mercies received, and which we are receiving.

Our family being now gathered together (those of us that were living), the South Church in Boston hired a house for us. Then we removed from Mr. Shepard's, those cordial friends, and went to Boston, where we continued about three quarters of a year. Still the Lord went along with us, and provided graciously for us. I thought it somewhat strange to set up house-keeping with bare walls, but as Solomon sayes, money answers all things, and that we had through the benevolence of Christian friends, some in this town, and some in that, and others, and some from England, that in a little time we might look, and see the house furnished with love. The Lord hath been exceeding good to us in our low estate, in that when we had neither house nor home, nor other necessaries, the Lord so moved the hearts of these and those towards us that we wanted neither food, nor raiment for ourselves or ours, Proverbs 18:24, "There is a friend which sticketh closer than a brother." And how many such friends have we found, and are now living amongst? And truly such a friend have we found him to be unto us, in whose house we lived, viz., Mr. James Whitcomb, a friend unto us near hand, and afar off.

I can remember the time, when I used to sleep quietly without workings in my thoughts, whole nights together, but now it is other wayes with me. When all are fast about me, and no eye open, but His who ever waketh, my thoughts are upon things past, upon the awfull dispensation of the Lord towards us, upon His wonderfull power and might, in carrying us through so many difficulties, in returning us to safety, and suffering none to hurt us. I remember in the night season, how the other day I was in the midst of thousands of enemies, & nothing but death before me. It was then hard work to perswade my self, that ever I should be satisfied with bread again. But now we are fed with the finest of the wheat, and, as I may say, with honey out of the rock. In stead of the husk, we have the fatted calf. The thoughts of these things in the particulars of them, and of the love and goodness of God towards us, makes it true of me, what David said to himself, Psalm 6:5, "I watered my couch with my tears." Oh! the wonderfull power of God that mine eyes have seen, affording matter enough for my thoughts to run in, that when others are sleeping mine eyes are weeping. I have seen the extreme vanity of this world: one hour I have been in health, and wealth, wanting nothing, but the next hour in sickness, and wounds, and death, having nothing but sorrow and affliction.

Before I knew what affliction meant, I was ready sometimes to wish for it. When I lived in prosperity;,having the comforts of the world about me, my relations by me, my heart cheerfull, and taking little care for anything, and yet seeing many, whom I preferred before myself, under many tryals and afflictions, in sickness, weakness, poverty, losses, crosses, and cares of the world, I should be sometimes jealous least I should have my portion in this life. And that scripture would come to my mind, Hebrews 12:6, "For whom the Lord loveth He chasteneth, and scourgeth every son whom He receiveth." But now I see the Lord had His time to scourge and chasten me. The portion of some is to have their affliction by drops, now one drop and then another, but the dregs of the cup, the wine of astonishment, like a sweeping rain that leaveth no food, did the Lord prepare to be my portion. Affliction I wanted, and affliction I had, full measure (I thought) pressed down and running over. Yet I see, when God calls a person to anything, and through never so many difficulties, yet He is fully able to carry them through and make them see, and say they have been gainers thereby. And I hope I can say in some measure, as David did, it is good for me that I have been afflicted. The Lord hath shewed me the vanity of these outward things. That they are the vanity of vanities, and vexation of spirit, that they are but a shadow, a blast, a bubble, and things of no continuance. That we must rely on God Himself, and our whole dependence must be upon Him. If trouble from smaller matters begin to arise in me, I have something at hand to check my self with, and say, "Why am I troubled?" It was but the other day that if I had had the world, I would have given it for my freedom, or to have been a servant to a Christian. I have learned to look beyond present and smaller troubles, and to be quieted under them, as Moses said, Exodous 14:13, "Stand still and see the salvation of the Lord."

FINIS.

Other titles from American Eagle Publications include:

The Day of Doom, By Michael Wigglesworth, the great Puritan epic
poem about the day of judgement, one of the most
influential books ever published in America.

The Hawks of Hawk Hollow, By Robert Montgomery Bird, an
exciting novel about the revolution, originally
published in 1835.

The Plays of Robert Munford, *The Candidates* and *The Patriots*. The
Oldest Comic Plays Written in America, dating back
to the 1780's.

The Little Black Book of Computer Viruses, a fascinating exposé of
how computer viruses work, including source code
for four different viruses.

For a free descriptive catalog, write to:

American Eagle Publications, Inc.
Post Office Box 41401-K
Tucson, Arizona 85717